This cute animals coloring book
belongs to :

____

cute cat

cat

brown bear

Bear

Little bird

Little Bird

cute doggy

Dog

Little tiger

Tiger

sand castle crab

sand castle crab

Honey bear

Honey Bear

Little Lion king

Lion

Hungry squirrel

squirrel

sleepy cat

sleepy cat

Little elephant

Elephant

Octopus and fishes

Octopus and fishes

cute ostrich

Ostrich

chicken farm

Chicken

Lotus frog

Lotus frog

Little giraffe

Giraffe

cow in farm

Cow in Farm

Fox in snow

Fox in snow

Piggy farm

piggy farm

cute rabbit

Rabbit

western horse

Horse

Delta hippo

Hippo

Pink flamingo

Flamingo

Night owl

Owl

cute little monkey

Monkey

smiley koala

Koala

Pacific whale

Whale

little sheep

Sheep

Bonus

Adventure

Bonus

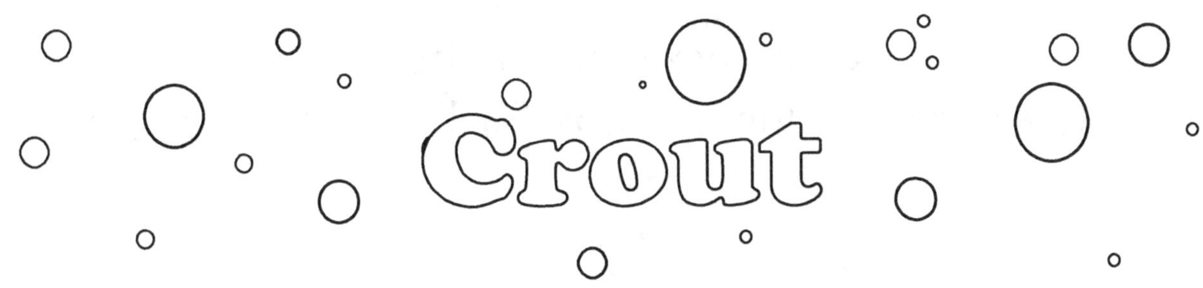
Crout